P9-CKB-402

Michelle Edwards

BLESSED ARE YOU

Traditional Everyday Hebrew Prayers

WITHDRAWN

Contra Costa County Library

JAN 4 1994

3 1901 01849 9493

LOTHROP, LEE & SHEPARD BOOKS   NEW YORK

To Meera, Flory, and Lelia

The author wishes to thank Dr. Joseph Lowin
for the transliterations of the prayers and
for his invaluable assistance with this book.
Thanks also to Rabbi Stacy Offner for all her help.

A Note from the Author

Blessed Are You is a book of everyday Hebrew prayers. When ocean waves tickle your toes, when thunder claps and lightning flashes in the sky, when you're tasting fresh challah or celebrating a birthday—all of these can be times for prayer. The children in this book are not shown praying because remembering God is part of their everyday lives.

This book is filled with pictures about three children and the things they do. There is no written story to go with the pictures, but each picture tells a story without words. As I worked on this book, I named the older two children Devra and David Levy, and I made them twins. I named their baby brother Jacob. I imagined that Devra and David had taught Jacob how to walk, and now they were trying to teach him how to talk. I liked to think that Devra loved flowers and the big blue sea better than anything, and that David loved animals, especially rabbits and birds. And I just knew that when his pet rabbit, Fluff, died, he was sadder than he ever thought he could be.

Devra and David know all the prayers in this book. I hope that you will learn some of them too, so that when something new and wonderful happens to you, you too can say: *Barukh ata, adonai eloheinu, melekh ha-olam, sheh-hecheyanu vekiy'manu ve-higiyanu laz'man ha-zeh.*

How to Use This Book

The original Hebrew prayer appears in the upper part of the text frame on each left-hand page. It should be read from right to left. My translation of the prayer is placed in the middle of the frame. The transliteration of the Hebrew is at the bottom and should be read from left to right.

The translations I have used in this book are my own, the ones I use with my children. You can find the literal translations in any traditional prayer book. Below you will find all the prayers in the order in which they appear in the book, followed by an explanation of their traditional uses.

1. **Thank You, God of everything, for the morning, when I wake again to You.**

   This prayer, called *Modeh Ahnee*, can be used as a morning prayer. Please note that the transliteration begins with *Modeh*. This indicates a masculine speaker. A feminine speaker would begin with *Modah*.

2. **Blessed are You, our God, Ruler of the universe. We thank You for the bread which comes from the seeds which grow in the earth that You created.**

   This prayer, known as *Ha-Motzi*, is said before eating bread.

3. **Blessed are You, our God, Ruler of the universe. Your strength and power fill our world.**

   This prayer is said upon seeing lightning and hearing thunder.

4. **Blessed are You, our God, Ruler of the universe, Who made the big and beautiful sea.**

   This prayer is said upon seeing the ocean or sea.

5. **Blessed are You, our God, Ruler of the universe, Who help me when I am sad and tired.**

   This prayer is said when comfort is needed.

6. **God, grant us peace and goodness, blessing and grace, kindness and mercy.**

   This is a prayer for peace.

7. **Blessed are You, our God, Ruler of the universe, Who created the fruit of the tree.**

   This prayer is said before eating fruit that grows on trees.

בָּרוּךְ אַתָּה

8. **Blessed are You, our God, Ruler of the universe, Who created all kinds of wonderful foods for us to eat.**

This prayer is said before eating baked goods other than bread.

9. **Blessed are You, our God, Ruler of the universe, for bringing us this special time and for the special things we enjoy.**

This prayer is said for first fruits, new experiences, and joyous occasions.

10. **Blessed are You, our God, Ruler of the universe. Thank You for creating our world with beauty big and small everywhere.**

This prayer is said upon seeing the beauties of nature.

11. **God bless my mother and my father.**

A prayer for parents.

12. **Blessed are You, our God, Ruler of the universe, Who made the wonders of creation.**

This prayer is said upon seeing the wonders of nature.

13. **Hear, O Israel, Adonai our God, Adonai is One.**

This prayer is called the *Sh'ma* (Listen) and is very important, for it states a belief in one God. It is sometimes used as a bedtime prayer.

מוֹדֶה אֲנִי לְפָנֶיךָ מֶלֶךְ חַי וְקַיָּם
שֶׁהֶחֱזַרְתָּ בִּי נִשְׁמָתִי בְּחֶמְלָה רַבָּה אֱמוּנָתֶךָ.

Thank You, God of everything,
for the morning,
when I wake again
to You.

Modeh ani lefanẹkha, mẹlekh chai vekayam,
sheh-hechezạrta bi nishmati be-chemla, raba emunatẹkha.

בָּרוּךְ אַתָּה, יְיָ אֱלֹהֵינוּ, מֶלֶךְ הָעוֹלָם, הַמּוֹצִיא
לֶחֶם מִן הָאָרֶץ.

Blessed are You, our God,
Ruler of the universe.
We thank You for the bread
which comes from the seeds
which grow in the earth
that You created.

Barukh ata, adonai eloheinu, melekh ha-olam,
ha-motzi lechem min ha-aretz.

בָּרוּךְ אַתָּה, יְיָ אֱלֹהֵינוּ, מֶלֶךְ הָעוֹלָם, שֶׁכֹּחוֹ
וּגְבוּרָתוֹ מָלֵא עוֹלָם.

Blessed are You, our God,
Ruler of the universe.
Your strength and power
fill our world.

Barukh ata, adonai eloheinu, melekh ha-olam,
sheh-kocho u-g'vurato maleh olam.

בָּרוּךְ אַתָּה, יְיָ אֱלֹהֵינוּ, מֶלֶךְ הָעוֹלָם, שֶׁעָשָׂה אֶת־הַיָּם הַגָּדוֹל.

B lessed are You, our God,
Ruler of the universe,
Who made the big
and beautiful sea.

Barukh ata, adonai elohẹinu, mẹlekh ha-olam,
sheh-assa et ha-yam ha-gadol.

בָּרוּךְ אַתָּה, יְיָ אֱלֹהֵינוּ, מֶלֶךְ הָעוֹלָם הַנּוֹתֵן לַיָּעֵף כֹּחַ.

Blessed are You, our God,
Ruler of the universe,
Who help me
when I am sad
and tired.

Barukh ata, adonai eloheinu, melekh ha-olam,
ha-noten la-ya'ef koach.

שִׂים שָׁלוֹם, טוֹבָה וּבְרָכָה, חֵן וָחֶסֶד
וְרַחֲמִים, עָלֵינוּ וְעַל כָּל יִשְׂרָאֵל עַמֶּךָ.

G od, grant us peace and goodness,
blessing and grace,
kindness and mercy.

Sim shalom, tova u-v'rakha, chen va-chessed
ve-rachamim, aleinu ve-al kol yisra'el amehkha.

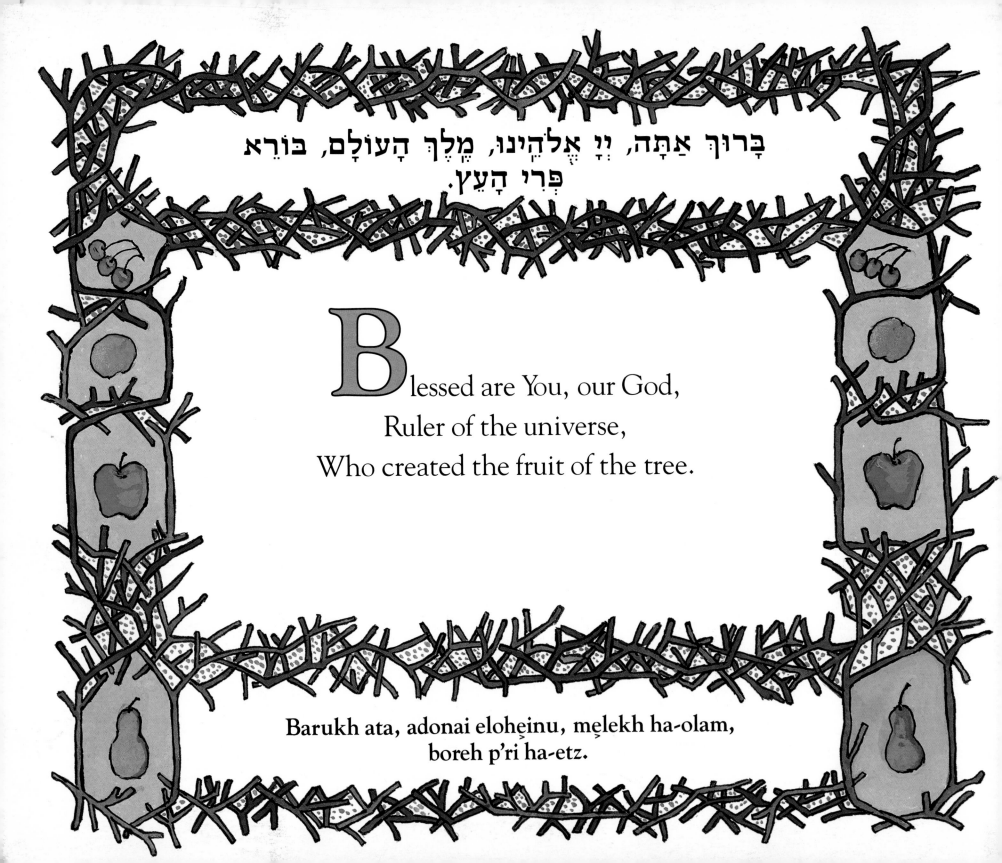

בָּרוּךְ אַתָּה, יְיָ אֱלֹהֵינוּ, מֶלֶךְ הָעוֹלָם, בּוֹרֵא פְּרִי הָעֵץ.

B lessed are You, our God,
Ruler of the universe,
Who created the fruit of the tree.

Barukh ata, adonai eloheinu, melekh ha-olam,
boreh p'ri ha-etz.

בָּרוּךְ אַתָּה, יְיָ אֱלֹהֵינוּ, מֶלֶךְ הָעוֹלָם, בּוֹרֵא מִינֵי מְזוֹנוֹת.

Blessed are You, our God, Ruler of the universe, Who created all kinds of wonderful foods for us to eat.

Barukh ata, adonai eloheinu, melekh ha-olam, boreh minei mezonot.

בָּרוּךְ אַתָּה, יְיָ אֱלֹהֵינוּ, מֶלֶךְ הָעוֹלָם, שֶׁהֶחֱיָנוּ וְקִיְּמָנוּ וְהִגִּיעָנוּ לַזְּמַן הַזֶּה.

B lessed are You, our God,
Ruler of the universe,
for bringing us this special time
and for the special things
we enjoy.

Barukh ata, adonai eloheinu, melekh ha-olam,
sheh-hecheyanu vekiy'manu ve-higiyanu laz'man ha-zeh.

בָּרוּךְ אַתָּה, יְיָ אֱלֹהֵינוּ, מֶלֶךְ הָעוֹלָם, שֶׁכָּכָה לוֹ, בְּעוֹלָמוֹ.

Blessed are You, our God,
Ruler of the universe.
Thank You for creating our world
with beauty
big and small
everywhere.

Barukh ata, adonai eloheinu, melekh ha-olam,
sheh-kacha lo be-olamo.

הָרַחֲמָן הוּא יְבָרֵךְ אֶת אָבִי מוֹרִי וְאֶת אִמִּי
מוֹרָתִי.

God bless my mother and my father.

Ha-rachaman hu yevarekh et avi mori ve-et immi morati.

בָּרוּךְ אַתָּה, יְיָ אֱלֹהֵינוּ, מֶלֶךְ הָעוֹלָם, עֹשֶׂה מַעֲשֵׂה בְּרֵאשִׁית.

Blessed are You, our God,
Ruler of the universe,
Who made the wonders
of creation.

Barukh ata, adonai eloheinu, melekh ha-olam, osseh
ma'asseh b'reishit.

שְׁמַע, יִשְׂרָאֵל, אֲדֹנָי אֱלֹהֵינוּ, אֲדֹנָי אֶחָד.

H

ear, O Israel,
Adonai our God,
Adonai is One.

Sh'ma, yisra'el, adonai eloḥeinu, adonai echad.

The paintings in this book were done in watercolor, gouache,
and colored pencil on B. F. K. Rives.

Copyright © 1993 by Michelle Edwards
All rights reserved. No part of this book may be reproduced or utilized in any form or by any means, electronic or mechanical, including photocopying and recording, or by any information storage and retrieval system, without permission in writing from the Publisher. Inquiries should be addressed to Lothrop, Lee & Shepard Books, a division of William Morrow & Company, Inc., 1350 Avenue of the Americas, New York, New York 10019. Printed in the United States of America.

First Edition   1   2   3   4   5   6   7   8   9   10

Library of Congress Cataloging in Publication
Edwards, Michelle. Blessed are you : traditional Jewish prayers for children / by Michelle Edwards.
p.   cm.   Summary: Prayers in transliterated Hebrew and English. ISBN 0-688-10759-1   1. Jewish children—Prayer-books and devotions—English.   2. Jewish children—Prayer-books and devotions—Hebrew.   3. Judaism—Prayer-books and devotions—English.
4. Judaism—Prayer-books and devotions—Hebrew.   [1. Prayers.   2. Judaism—Prayer books and devotions.]   I. Title.   BM666.E34
1993   296.4—dc20   92-1666   CIP   AC